Hugh and I

A short story by Brian J. Ek

Foreword

All too often we tend to think of our past and remember things that were often disappointing or bad. But I recall a time in my life where I was happy and content spending time with my father-in-law, Hugh Peabody. Hugh was a gentle and kind person who seldom thought of himself and enjoyed the simple things in life.

Hugh didn't come from a well-to-do family and he had to work hard to support his family as most of do. It wasn't until I married his daughter Keri that I came to know more about him and wanted more than ever to keep learning.

We both shared memories and stories together of our favorite times and not so favorite times in life and I believe this brought us closer together in our relationship. He and his wife Nancy spent sixty years together and even though I was only to share some of those years, they were years that I will cherish forever.

This book shares some of my greatest memories with my best friend Hugh. I hope you enjoy this book as much as I did in writing it.

Sometimes in life you run into a relationship that totally astounds you and makes your life better knowing that person and the impact that they make on your life. Once such person has become my best friend and companion and his name is Hugh Peabody.

I came to know Hugh when I was dating his daughter Keri while I was in high school. He was a very caring father as I recall. He was slow to be upset and to me he didn't seem to have too many cares about anything other than his family.

He was a hard working man, working for a local farmer accomplishing many tasks throughout each day. And I remember countless times sharing a meal, talks and games with him as I grew up in those days.

I recall going to family functions with his family and to church on many occasions. He was just an all-around nice man.

It wasn't until 25 years after I left high school that I married his daughter Keri that I really got to know the man I would call my best friend.

I searched out Keri after having a failed marriage and she and I began our courtship. I wasn't sure that Hugh remembered me, although his wife Nancy stated that she did. Probably because he wasn't always around for my visits with their daughter and Nancy was.

Even though Hugh didn't totally remember those high school days of mine, he still accepted me with open arms. I even recall one visit later in life that just before leaving that he gave me a hug to say goodbye.

It wasn't until a few years after I married Keri that Hugh and I became best friends. I had asked Hugh if he'd like to go fishing and he replied that he didn't have a fishing license. I asked him if he had a license if he would go fishing with me and he said "yes".

So I took him up to the local "Holiday" store and got him a license. We also picked up some worms and a couple pops and proceeded to go find a local fishing hole.

In the immediate Cambridge, Minnesota area there are lots of lakes within just a few miles from each other. The one we picked was just east of a little town called Grandy. I believe it was named "Twin Lakes" as there was a lake on either side of the road. Back then a person could park on either side of the road and set up a chair or two and drop lines in the water.

Hugh and I would sit out there for hours and even if it rained, I always came prepared with either and umbrella or disposable rain gear. Sometimes we would catch a bunch of fish and sometimes we wouldn't get a bite, but it really didn't matter as we were spending time in the great outdoors together.

Hugh and I would talk about the clouds as they formed or we'd talk about an Eagle nesting in the nearby trees. It really didn't make much of a difference if we were catching fish or not. It was just great being together and sharing each other's time with one another.

I recall one time while fishing at "Twin Lakes" that a thunderstorm came up on us rather fast and both of us jumped into the car as torrential downpours came upon us. Everyone else that had been fishing decided to leave, but Hugh and I waited the storm out.

I would turn on the car and warm and dry us out and we'd just talk about the rain and whether or not we could see which way the storm was headed and if we'd see the end of the storm clouds approaching.

And just as soon as the clouds would pass, he and I would be back outside, cleaning off our chairs and fishing once again.

For me, it was heaven on earth. We'd fish and talk for hours upon end. Every once in a while I'd get a call on my cell phone from my wife or Hugh's wife asking where we were at and if we were planning on coming home for supper anytime soon. We both chuckled when that happened.

Maybe we were spending too much time fishing. We both thought "not"!

There were days that went by when we hadn't been out for a while do to work or other obligations but I'd call Hugh and say, "I've got the day off tomorrow, how about we grab breakfast at McDonald's and then find a new spot for fishing". Hugh would most of time say yes to that.

At some point in our relationship, I started calling Hugh, Dad. He was my Dad through marriage, so it was fitting and he didn't suggest anything otherwise.

Dad would sometimes call and ask what I was doing and sometimes I'd say that I had to work and I could tell he was disappointed somewhat. But other times I'd say I'll be over to pick him up shortly.

One day while out fishing near Stanchfield, I asked Dad if he'd be okay with fishing from a boat. He said that would be fine. So I went online to Amazon and ordered a twelve foot inflatable boat. And we set out on our first adventure on Lake Florence.

I remember the day was a bit breezy and soon enough we ended up at the east end of the lake.

It had gotten quite windy and all that I had to propel the boat was a couple of oars. I wouldn't let Dad use them though as he was in his 70's and I was only in my mid 40's. It took all of my strength to get us back to the boat launch and I was exhausted.

I told Dad that I was going to make some changes before we set out on another excursion. So that next day I went to Wal-Mart, and purchased a trolling motor and battery. Then I got on Amazon again and ordered a transom mount and an anchor.

Soon after our fishing excursions became a lot easier. It would generally take Dad and me about 20 minutes to inflate the boat and get all the gear into the boat.

I remember joking around in the boat and I was taking a few photos with my phone. Dad posed for one. The photo looked like he was about to eat a worm. I sent that one via a message to Keri and her reply was "yuck". Dad and I did a lot of crazy things like that.

One morning while out on Lake Florence, we came across an inlet to what must have been another lake that I hadn't known about. Dad knew there was another lake adjacent to Lake Florence, but it must have slipped his mind. The inlet was very shallow and we had to pull up the trolling motor and navigate the channel with just a paddle.

Once we were able to coast through to the other side we found a plethora of Sunfish and Crappies waiting for us. Dad and I talked about how many weeds were in the lake and how we hoped we wouldn't get our lines caught on them, but really, we didn't care too much about that.

We were pretty happy to have made it onto the new lake and were like a couple of kids in a candy store when we did.

Some days, I'd pack a lunch and we'd spend all day fishing on those lakes. Dad would talk about times growing up in the area and things that he and his siblings would do to occupy their time when not helping their parents on the farm.

I became more interested in hearing about those days and sometimes I would recall the things I used to do when I was a child.

Fishing was in my blood. I recall my own Dad and siblings going on fishing trips and talking about the "big one" that got away.

Some trips with Hugh were pretty easy and some were difficult, depending on what lakes we chose to explore. Some we couldn't access by boat and could only fish from shore. But that really didn't matter to us too much as long as we were spending time together.

While at my work at a residential treatment center one day, I had a small stroke and I landed up in the hospital for several weeks. And after recouping from it, I was going crazy at home doing nothing, and all I could think of was going fishing with Dad.

My doctor really didn't want me to go back to work or exert myself in anyway. He wanted me to relax as much as I could. And I couldn't think of a better way than fishing therapy with my best friend Hugh.

The other thing my doctor didn't want me doing was driving. I explained to the doctor that if I was going to be able to relax, that I would have to drive to one of our many favorite fishing holes. So the doctor gave me permission to drive.

I'm sure I was driving my wife "crazy" being cooped up at home all the time. And I didn't want her to worry about me and I'm sure she didn't as long as I had my phone with me and her father by my side.

My therapy was having her Dad with me doing what we loved doing and that of course was fishing.

Dad and I spent the next several weeks fishing from shore as it was a little too difficult for me to be lifting the boat and dragging it to the lake. Little things "tired" me out more than it used to. So Dad and I would spend many a day fishing on the Rum River in the Cambridge Park. We didn't catch much of anything other than small Sunnies or bass. But again, we really didn't care. We had plenty of things to talk about.

Sometimes Dad and I would just sit and enjoy the weather or the scenery. It didn't make any difference to us as long as we were sharing time together.

Dad and I didn't always get out to fish. We also enjoyed doing other things together. We both live in "Pine Village" mobile home park, which is a park for those fifty-five years of age and older.

Dad decided one day to build a roof over the front of his house and I offered to help. I was not the best help he could have chosen, but at least I offered to help. My building skills were greatly inefficient back in those days, but I wanted to help and maybe gain some knowledge from my old friend.

He measured and I cut the two by fours to length and helped attach them to the side of the house. I learned a great deal from helping and it also helped when it came to making repairs on my own homes as well.

Dad taught me basic electrical, wood building and other key essentials to up-keeping a home. I got some well acquainted with these skills, that I now am able to perform these deeds adequately in and around my own home.

Dad taught me how to be patient when working on projects and how to rely on my own skills to save money and build equity in my home.

Later, I asked him to help me with various projects around my home as well.

Sure, we'd still find time to go fishing, but it really didn't make any difference to me as long as I got to spend quality time with him.

Dad started showing signs of aging as we all do and some days I'd call and see if he was up for fishing and he wasn't. Sometimes he just wasn't feeling up to par. Other days I'd be working and didn't have time for him. I'd feel bad, but life continues on.

Many of the lakes we visited really didn't have names you'll find on maps, but still had local names. We'd fished on quite a few of those and a few that did have names like, Fannie, Green Lake, Rush Lake, Skogman, Lake Francis, and Long Lake.

We did venture out further some times to lakes that were more than 30 miles away like Blue Lake.

Driving on the back roads of rural central Minnesota is really nice if you ever just get the gumption to do. Some of the scenery is breath-taking and some of the villages and smaller towns are really unique and sometimes you never really new they were there. It's truly an adventure!

I recall another time when we were fishing at Twin Lakes just outside of Grandy when Dad hooked a huge snapping turtle. He pulled and pulled on the line and got it in close to shore, but the line broke just at the time when we could see how big he was.

After that we started carrying along his old rod and reel with the heavy "rope" line as I called it and a garden spade, just in case either of us would hook up with another snapper that size.

I remember my grandfather catching a mammoth snapper and grandma making snapper stew from it. Ah, the good old days of my childhood. Memories like those are hard to come by, that's for sure. It's too bad that today's kids couldn't gain memories like I did when I was a child. I digress.

Dad and I had a lot of great times each year journeying to different spots to go fishing. I complained a lot though when it came to lakes with so many weeds and then I would start crabbing about how the DNR had so much money that they should start using it to clean up those lakes instead of making more rules for their books.

I picked up one of those fishing rule books and it's gotten to be to the point where it's not as much fun fishing as much as it used to be. Too many rules and regulations I would say. Dad wouldn't get too involved during my rants. He's just sat and listened and then I'd be done. He didn't seem to have a care in the world.

Sometimes we would be driving and Dad would recall some of the places he used to deliver propane. I learned a lot about some of the back roads and pathways he'd taken in years past.

Some of those roads had ponds on them, so we'd stop and fish from those as well.

Dad and I went fishing on Green Lake on morning and witnessed a guy and his wife loading a nice boat from the local launch. She had a video camera in hand and placed it on the dock as he brought his boat to the water. He had so many rods and reels that I lost count.

I inquired about them and he introduced himself as Tim Horton. He was I believe from Alabama and he had a nationally televised fishing show called, "Tim Horton Outdoors".

Dad and I couldn't believe the size and style of the boat and how much electronics it had and the motor was huge. It was really cool to see. This guy fished Green Lake on several occasions and stated that Minnesota was one of his favorite states to fish in.

Dad and I watched him get on the boat with his wife and then take off to the middle of the lake within what seemed like seconds. It was truly a sight to see.

Shortly after the boat left, Dad hooked a big one. It was so big, that I had him pose with it for the cover of this book. That was pretty much all either one of us caught that day.

But all in all, we had another great day joking around with each other and doing what we both loved.

We sure had many great times while out fishing together.

Dad and I took a young man out fishing one day. He was the son of my wife Keri's friend Nancy Hasseth. His name is Andrew.

Dad and I explained to Andrew that there were certain things that needed to be done prior to dropping your bobber in the water, like learning to whisper. Andrew asked why we needed to whisper. I replied that fish could hear really well and the sound of our voice amplified while in the boat and that the boat was like a "loudspeaker".

So Andrew starting whispering and dropped his bobber in the water and low and behold caught the first of many fish that day. He of course was the only lucky one to land any either. It didn't mean too much to Dad and I as we'd caught fish before, but to Andrew it was great!

Andrew with his first fish of the day!

Andrew just kept on catching fish like this nice bass.

It was a pleasure for both Dad and I to have Andrew along on his first fishing trip in the boat.

Andrew never went along with Dad and me again, but Andrew and I have gone out a few more times together, mainly fishing off of shore.

One day Dad and I were fishing the Rum River near the Springvale Township. We were sitting at the boat launch talking away as I cast my line in the water and within seconds I got a huge hit on my line. I saw the fish jump out of the water and thought to myself that it must be a Carp that I've hooked.

I started reeling my line in and the fish put up quite a fight. I finally got the fish into shore and low and behold what I thought was a Carp was instead about a 9 pound Northern Pike!

Both Dad and I looked at it in amazement. It was huge! Unfortunately it swallowed the hook and was bleeding profusely.

Dad and I were "catch and release" fishermen and I felt so bad that this fish was going to die. Then Dad told me that possibly an animal would feed on it if I let it go down river. With him having said that, I released it and watched it float down river.

I hoped that a bear or something would have a feast on the big one. After sending it down river, I said to Dad, "I didn't even get a picture of it to prove that I caught a big one".

Oh well, Dad replied. It'll be just another fish story then. We both chuckled at the statement.

If I had to think of the best fishing hole that Dad and I fished, it would have to be Long Lake on the west side near Captain's on Long Lake. There was a boat launch there and seldom used as it was gated off and not open very often except for special times.

We really didn't catch that much fish there, but I do remember catching a Bullhead there and throwing it back in the lake and then watching an Eagle swoop down and grab it. That was amazing! Dad and I talked about that for weeks.

We'd talk about the small speed boats going by and then which direction the clouds seemed to be going. Several times I remember planes flying overhead and Dad identifying some of them.

Sometimes we'd cast over each other's lines and get them tangled terribly. But not to worry though, as I always had plenty of extra fishing line with me.

I can't tell you how many times I'd lose a bobber in that lake. Someone could probably open up a store from all that I lost.

Whether it was sunny or raining, it wasn't a care to us as we were having fun. But sometimes it got to be just too hot, so we'd try our luck another day.

A few years earlier, I met a guy by the name of Dan Gapen, who was a fishing aficionado and inventor of fishing lures. I hosted a local radio show in Princeton and on Friday's Dan would come in and share his time and experience with the listeners.

One day he brought a huge box of different lures to giveaway while I fished with Dad at local lakes around the area. One of the lures was called the "Spin Bee".

This lure caught me more Sunfish than I've ever caught in my life and I shared lures with Dad. Some of the lures were rather large and we joked about using them one day, however, we never did.

I told Dan that I would hand out a business card with every lure and he was agreeable with that. I'm pretty sure that everyone that got a "Spin Bee" caught some incredible fish, as Dad and I always did.

That was surely a fun summer fishing and giving goodies away at the lake.

Dad and I continue to fish went the time presents itself. We usually stop for breakfast and coffee before heading out for the day and sometimes we take a break and do some sight-seeing on the back roads of rural Minnesota. It's a time that's enjoyable for both of us.

We've met so many anglers and people from all over the states that it's never a dull moment.

We've heard stories including some fish stories about fishing the local lakes and some of those stories weren't even about fishing, but we enjoyed them all the same.

If you have a young person or you're an older guy like me, I urge you to build lasting memories with someone you care for by getting out and fishing some of the greatest lakes in your area. Enjoy those folks in your lives and make an impact on someone in your life as Hugh has made on mine.

In 2019 Dad had a couple small strokes, one of which affected some of his speech and memory. I pray that he will overcome these issues and we can continue to make precious memories fishing and other antics.

Hugh and Nancy Peabody during their 60th wedding anniversary in 2019.

I appreciate the times Dad and I have been able to spend together. Having said this, I dedicate this short story to my best friend and adventurer, Hugh Roger Peabody.

Hugh, you are a great father-in-law, confidant and friend and I will always cherish the memories of fishing with my best friend Hugh!

He told me one morning when I went to sit with him that he was only going to be around for another month. That morning instead of us going fishing, and stopping at McDonald's for breakfast and senior coffees, I brought him breakfast. He and I sat down at the table to share one last breakfast. It almost felt as though he was saying "goodbye" in his own unique way.

Hugh (Dad) passed away in the early afternoon on December 22, 2020. It was hard to see him go, but I'm happy that he's no longer in pain. My life was better with him in my life. I know that I will cherish his friendship along with the knowledge I gained from him in the short time that I knew him.

This book is dedicated to my best friend. To you Dad, I will always remember that when I'm feeling down that I can just remember the great times we shared together, just you and me.

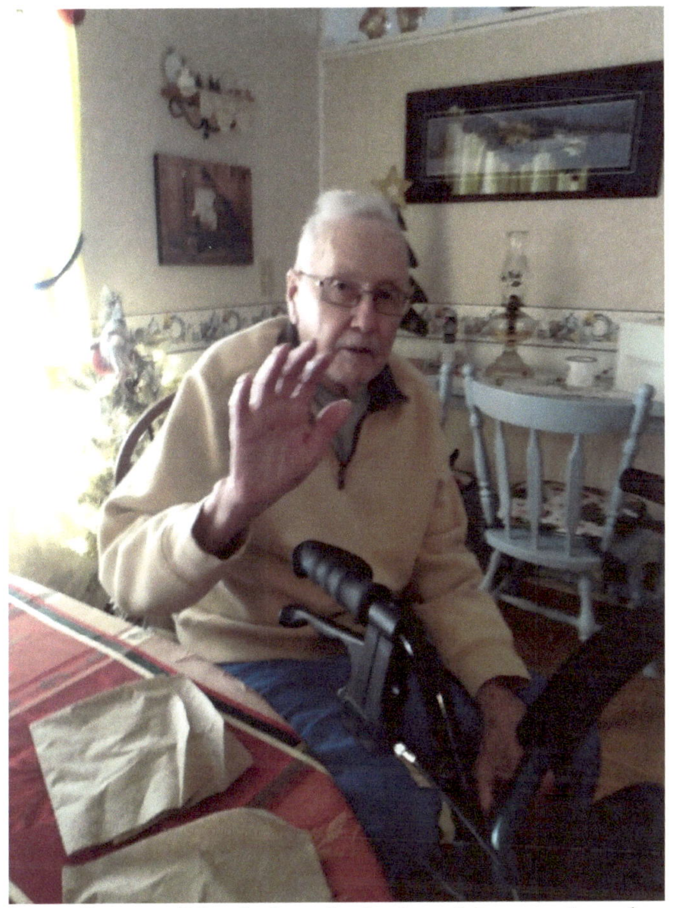

The last photo of Dad shortly before his passing, he was actually getting his picture taken to use in a text message to his daughter, my wife Keri, just to say hello.

As I'm sitting at my computer this morning, December 23, 2020, and updating my book about him, I decided to add a few extra photos of him to share with those that knew him, his children, friends and neighbors and others. The next several pages are of Dad and the people he loved.

The Peabody's

HAPPY
EASTER

CHISAGO CO. FAIR
Come Show Your

© 2020 Brian J. Ek